Gifts
of the
Lotus

The mandala is recognized throughout the world as a symbol of wholeness. The three lotus pads which comprise a portion of this mandala symbolize the trinity, or the trinitarian nature of man. The lotus itself represents the unfoldment of consciousness as it evolves toward its true nature. The gold star is a simple archetypal figure frequently found in a mandala.

Gifts of the Lotus

Compiled by **Virginia Hanson**

This publication made possible with the assistance of the Kern Foundation.

The Theosophical Publishing House
Wheaton, Ill. / Madras, India / London, England

Library of Congress Cataloging in Publication Data

Hanson, Virginia, comp.
    Gifts of the Lotus
    (A Quest original)
    1. Devotional calendars.   I. Title
    BL624.H3   242'.2   74-5130
    ISBN 0-8356-0450-0

Printed in the United States of America

TABLE OF CONTENTS

(Compiler's Note: In order not to distract attention from the ideas being presented, the sources of the separate daily meditations are listed at the end of the book rather than immediately following the individual quotations.)

INTRODUCTION

Modern man, in his search for meaning, has rediscovered the ancient science of meditation. Meditative practice has become as necessary a part of life for the businessman as for the artist and mystic. Both the man of action and the man of thought have found in this most noble of arts the key to understanding the nature of the inner self and to awakening the inherent capacities of the fully human, and consequently humane, individual.

Because man is also, by his very nature, a symbol-maker, investing the objects in the world about him with meaningfulness, he seeks, through symbols, to comprehend the underlying unity of life, its interconnectedness, and its beauty of purpose. Among the most significant of symbols, held sacred from remotest antiquity, has been the lotus. Revered in China and Japan, held sacred in ancient Egypt and India alike, adopted as a Christian emblem by the Greek and Latin Churches who replaced it by the water lily, the lotus has always typified the life of man and of the cosmos. Symbol of wisdom and of the liberation of the indwelling self, the lotus has been the emblem of the creative powers in the universe, both spiritual and physical. As the lotus-seed contains within itself a perfect miniature of the future plant, man has been reminded of the fact that the spiritual prototypes of all things exist in immaterial realms before their manifestation in physical existence.

The root of the lotus anchored in mud may be said to represent material existence; the stalk passing up through the water typifies our experience in the emotional realm; the flower floating on the water and opening to the sky is symbolic of the awakening of the spirit. So the symbol of the lotus, representing the emanation of the objective from the subjective, as well as the flowering of the human spirit in its longing for the Divine, signifies the possibility of man's achievement of wholeness, the union of his outer and inner nature in the service of the one universal life. Unfolding from within outward, the potentialities of the Immortal Self are revealed in the actualities of man's existential self; the lotus of the spirit opens on the tranquil waters of our psychological nature and our actions exhibit the harmony of the Divine.

The art of daily meditation reveals the lotus-nature of the Self—the Christ-

Self, the *Atman*—the immortal divine spark that lies entombed within the physical tabernacle. The royal road to the discovery of the gifts of that lotus-self lies, as it has from time immemorial, along the pathways of study, concentration, and contemplation to the supreme heights of illumination and liberation. The meditative thoughts in this small book may serve as guideposts along that royal road, encouraging the unfoldment of the Divine within the human heart, laying bare in the sunlight of the spirit the jeweled gifts of the lotus.

—Joy Mills

FREEDOM

1. Freedom is obedience to universal Law; and we feel most free when we obey the law of our own being. That law is within us and seeks expression through us.

∞

2. These are the six fetters of non-liberation. Where great faith is, is a way to freedom. To depend upon a wise, good Lama is a way to freedom. When pure precepts are kept, is a way to freedom. To dwell in solitude is a way to freedom. To remain alone is a

way to freedom. To practice meditation is a way to freedom.

∞

3. You shall be free indeed when your
days are not without a care nor your
nights without a want and a grief.
But rather when these things girdle
your life and yet you rise above them
naked and unbound.

∞

4. We are prisoned by our aloneness, but
liberated by our belonging to mankind. We are prisoned by our same-
ness to all men, but liberated by our
uniqueness. That both these things
are so is a paradox.

∞

5. The price of freedom, "hard-bought" indeed, is to live with the burden of our choices, to endure the painful process of self-loosening of the bonds we have put upon ourselves, to accept joyfully and willingly total responsibility for our thoughts, feelings, and actions. Perhaps it is only such acceptance of the burden of freedom that makes us finally truly and fully human.

∽

6. Our urgent need is to enlarge our awareness so that we transcend the crippling narrowness of egoism which blocks the realization of our true nature. Freedom is creative energy released within areas of limitation. Limitations are not fixed. No one

knows the power he has for freedom until he exercises it.

ॐ

7. ... this absolute command to duty proves at last the freedom of our wills; how could we ever have conceived such a notion as duty is we had not felt ourselves free? We cannot prove this freedom by theoretical reason; we prove it by feeling it directly in the crisis of moral choice.... In a way which we feel but cannot prove, each of us is free.

ॐ

8. He who is really free can wear any faith, or even stage or mode of living, and be his true self in it. He is free of

all modes and forms, for he has found the Life in all things.

❦

9. Man's will is a faculty of his inner higher human self. In this higher self ... are all the cosmic qualities and powers. Within himself, but deep within his inmost being, man is of this mighty stature. His efforts to move toward freedom will slowly unfold these latent powers and as he progresses he will shed his crippling limitations and move out into a state of freedom hardly dreamed of as yet by most of us.

❦

10. There seems to be a link between freedom and the complete understanding which can arise from a direct confrontation with the truth of things as they actually are, not as we would wish them to be or not to be.

❦

11. No matter how distorted our interpretations of freedom may be, if there were no such quality inherent in the universe, we could not misinterpret it. No one can claim indeterminacy for the atom and deny it in man.

❦

12. The moment of first free choice represents a new dimension in the

evolution of the soul, a pulling away from interminable eons of unself-conscious reaction.

∞

13. Putting off the body is not Freedom, any more than putting away one's staff and waterpot; but getting free from the knots of unwisdom in the heart—that is Freedom, in very deed.

∞

14. Free is he who is the same whether in full action or poised in stillness; who encountering emptiness or fulfillment, happiness or horror, hears the silent voice everywhere murmuring, "I, too, am God"—the voice of the Union of All.

∞

15. Freedom relates not only to man's social and economic life, but equally to his spiritual urges and longings, for without some satisfaction of these, he suffers from incompleteness.

༄

16. As a conscious being, man is free when he feels free. Freedom for him is truly an inner condition. It is freedom from psychological fetters. It is a state of psychological ease which is both self-contained, that is, un-wanting, and self-expressive.

༄

17. In a system that is unitary and therefore one in which there is an interrelatedness of all that exists, the

exercise of freedom cannot be separated from a responsibility for the results of that exercise.

❧

18. Freedom is fullest when ideal and real are in full accord. For there are degrees of freedom. Freedom is not only power to conceive, but also to carry out purposes.

❧

19. . . . the path of freedom becomes less attractive to many because they have wanted freedom as a personal possession, a convenient personal adjunct. And we cannot possess freedom. Freedom must possess us.

❧

20. We must determine whether we really want freedom—whether we are willing to dare the perils of continuous rebirth out of the old into the new, with all the grief and sense of loss this may seem to entail with every dying. For we never take a step forward without surrendering something that we may have held dear, without dying to that which has been.

❧

21. The spiritually free individual is one who has reached a harbor of tranquillity immune to the currents and stresses of ordinary living. He is not striving for freedom. He is free because of increased perception of the nature of the world.

❧

22. Freedom is manifested through a lawfulness of being. It is a release through action of universal principles.

∾

23. The four freedoms of the aspirant: To desist from possessions and security; the abolition of fear; the discovery of one's own way; and instinctive individual action.

∾

24. Freedom does not imply severance from the world; that severance means helplessness; and man is free not from his world but by means of his world. His world is the partner of his spiritual enterprise, and he achieves in the degree in which he liberates the

truest meaning and highest possibilities of the universe.

❧

25. Freedom is not a thing to be weighed and measured; it is a movement of the spirit, unimpeded, unhampered, without resistance, without barrier or obstruction to the flow of life itself.

❧

26. What appears to be needed to establish a consistent flow of psychic freedom is the acceptance of situations in constantly new and fresh frames of reference. . . . Whenever there is a sitting back and suffering; whenever there is a servile dependence upon his-

tory, there will we find bondage—a lack of free will.

ᴏᴡᴏ

27. Freedom is really a spiritual state, although it can be reflected at lesser levels. And it is only in freedom in the deepest sense that the riches of the Spirit can manifest themselves.

ᴏᴡᴏ

28. Freedom of the individual cannot be achieved in isolation but is intimately involved with the other deepest problems of human life. No man can strive after and gain this freedom alone and leave the other vital problems of life unsolved. It involves his

whole life and requires a total effort on his part.

๛

29. Freedom, then, lies only in our innate human capacity to choose between different sorts of bondage, bondage to desire and self-esteem, or bondage to the light that lightens all our lives. . . . Freely to choose to bind ourselves in ever increasing servitude to the Light eventually wins for us identity with the unlimited, the free.

๛

30. Freedom within oneself means that there is always free action, unforced, out of one's intelligence and free will, that is, without ever being involved in

or subject to forces that compel or determine one's action.

∾

31. Give freedom to the ones who dwell close to your heart, not by separating yourself from them, trying to draw apart, for that often holds them in closer bonds. Give freedom in every thought, give love—overflowing love—with no restriction in your mind, no question of any kind.

COMPASSION

1. Let thy Soul lend its ear to every cry of pain like as the lotus bares its heart to drink the morning sun. Let not the fierce Sun dry one tear of pain before thyself has wiped it from the sufferer's eye. But let each burning human tear drop on thy heart and there remain, nor ever brush it off, until the pain that caused it is removed.

∽

2. We have to create for ourselves a body of compassion in which our fellow-beings will be cells.

∽

3. We reach a point when we become satiated with ourselves and when life demands that we turn outward toward other human life. When we cease being the passive vessel and ourselves become the living spring.

❧

4. Let us remember this, as we turn aside from the wrong-doer: a happy person never yet has done wrong, and let us rather pity than condemn.

❧

5. When we are bound to another human being in triumph and disaster, we are lifted above the passions of pity and envy; his grief is our grief;

his joy is our joy; we are as one in a union of hearts.

ᏯᏬ

6. As a horse when he has run . . . a bee when it has made its honey, so a man when he has done a good act, does not call out for others to come and see, but he goes on to another act, as a vine goes on to produce again the grapes in season.

ᏯᏬ

7. From the myriads of men and women whose great gift is love of wife or husband, child or parent or friend, the Plan asks for deeds of tenderness and bravery, those seemingly trivial incidents of smile and touch of hand

which encourage another to go on his way unflinchingly to his goal.

∾

8. It is of the Lord's mercies that we are not consumed, because his compassions fail not. They are new every morning.

∾

9. The sense of Compassion has its lower and its higher aspects. In its lower aspects it exists more to avoid the personal discomfort of a vision of unhappiness and misery. Compassion in its higher aspect ascends from general kindness, through tenderness in protection and guidance, to the noble heights of passionate sympathy.

∾

10. Compassion is the fundamental law of Nature's own heart. It means becoming at one with the divine Universe, with the universal life and consciousness. It means harmony; it means peace; it means bliss; it means impersonal Love.

∼

11. Let us be kind. The love-power in so many of us is such a poor, cramped, egotistic copy of the Divine Flame. I think when we come to the last great Gateway, we shall be glad to remember that we have been kind, that we have encouraged, that we have forgiven.

∼

12. We must aim only at striving to channel better the love-power of the universe, that we may add to the sum total of happiness in this world and "try to lift a little of the heavy karma of the world."

∿

13. Human beings become humane beings only when they have learned to *feel with* others, for this is the meaning of compassion. It is the crown of consciousness marking the king among men; but it is a crown which any commoner may lift to his own head. That crown [does not] signify conquest or power over others, but conquest and power over the self,

than which there is no other real power or glory.

༄

14. When we have reached [the] sublime goal, we shall have the impulse to turn around, as do the glorious Buddhus of Compassion who turn backward on the Path, and help our fellows trailing along behind. This compassionate act is what all true spiritual saviors of men do.

༄

15. Pity comes from the infinite accumulations of man's memory, from the anguish, pain and suffering of life, from the full deposit of experience, from the forgotten faces, the lost

men, from the million strange and haunting visages of time. . . . It always comes most keenly from a little thing.

∾

16. Compassion is the very nature and fabric of the structure of the Universe itself . . . for compassion means "feeling with," and the Universe is an Organism, a vast and mighty organism, an organism without bounds, which might otherwise be called Universal Life-consciousness.

∾

17. The degree to which one is sensitive to other people's suffering, to other men's humanity, is the index of one's

own humanity. It is the root not only for social living but also of the study of humanities. The vital presupposition of the philosopher's question about man is his care for man.

❦

18. Help your needy brother and you shall be helped yourself, in virtue of the never failing and ever active Law of Compensation.

❦

19. Be yourself, and expand your sympathies; touch with the tendrils of your consciousness the hearts of other human beings. . . . Be kindly, refuse to hate. Let your heart expand.

❦

20. Pity and compassion are the proper feelings to cherish in respect to all erring humanity, and we must not give place to any other emotion, such as resentment, annoyance, or vexation.

ᕧ

21. By thinking of the story of my Guru,
    Reverence and faith grow from the
       bottom of my heart,
    Compassion and waves of grace enter
       into me.

ᕧ

22. Compassion is rooted in love. And harmony and love are fundamentally the same. Its very nature, the very structure of it, is that every part feels what every other part undergoes; and

this, in its higher reaches and when expressing itself in human hearts, men call compassion.

∽

23. A kindly thought sent out toward some other human being is a protection to that other, and it is a beautiful thing to do. It is a human thing, a truly human thing, and one that every normal human being loves to do.

∽

24. Never to judge rashly; never to interpret the actions of others in an ill-sense, but to compassionate their infirmities, bear their burdens, excuse their weaknesses, and make up for

their defects—this is the true spirit of charity.

∞

25. The term "Universal Brotherhood" is no idle phrase. . . . It is the only secure foundation for universal morality. If it be a dream, it is at least a noble one for mankind.

∞

26. We make ourselves to be exactly what we are; and we are, at the same time, our brothers' keepers, because each one of us, *each one of us,* is responsible for an aeonic chain of causation . . . we cannot think or speak or act without affecting other beings, to their weal or to their woe.

∞

27. Man achieves fullness of being in fellowship, in care for others. He expands his existence by "bearing his fellow-man's burden." As we have said, animals are concerned for their own needs; the degree of our being human stands in direct proportion of the degree in which we care for others.

∽

28. Compassion is no attribute. It is the Law of Laws—eternal Harmony, Alaya's Self; a shoreless universal essence, the light of everlasting Right, and fitness of all things, the law of love eternal.

∽

29. Cease to judge a movement, a cause, an opinion, by the extent to which it appeals to you, satisfies you, or perhaps antagonizes you. Examine rather the measure of its power to be of service to others in their need.

March

TRUTH

1. There are certain human biases that go into cosmic interpretation. We find in the cosmos the things that are in us....If it turns out that the cosmos is defined partly by the nature of what we are, so also we find out a lot more about ourselves by bringing ourselves into this two-way relation with the cosmos.

∾

2. I do not know what I may appear to the world; but to myself I seem to have been only like a boy playing on the seashore, and diverting myself in

now and then finding a smoother pebble or a prettier shell than ordinary, whilst the great ocean of truth lay all undiscovered about me.

&

3. Truth never descends to our world of error; he who would know it must ascend toward that world of Reality where he can see face to face and, for a while, become living truth. It is possible for man to know the mystery of life; solve it he never can, still less contain it in an intellectual system, however logical. Life is not logical, though logic is the alphabet which we must learn if we would speak the language of life, which is truth.

&

4. Nature lays no banquet of obvious truths for us at her table. That which we require to feed us must be dug out by ourself with blistered hands and aching head. Everything that is worth while is recondite, unobservable, and hard to come at.

∾

5. There is a truth in each thing, and that is the truth of its being, what it is in its essence, which may not be the same as what it appears to be, or even what it appears to do. It is this truth in ourselves which we have first to discover, before we can see the truth in others.

∾

6. In these silent places you receive illumination, you receive visions of truth, because your spirit—the core of you, the heart of you—has gone into the very core of being.

∽

7. To say that Truth as an absolute is beyond conception is not to say that truth as a reality is beyond experience. For it is inherent in experience and in the experiencer. It is the phoenix rising out of the ashes of its dead self, ever new and eternally existent. And every knowing, every moment of awareness of that rebirth, brings its own freedom.

∽

8. So let us seek the True, in everything, in everybody, in every circumstance, with patience, with humility, with love.

࿐

9. The leaders of the race should ever impress the average man with this: that there is no game or sport half as fascinating as the pursuit of truth, since truth is the basis of everything man hopes to make endure.

࿐

10. Truth in speech and truth in thought are very important. The more you can feel falsehood as being not part of yourself, as coming on you from

outside, the easier it will be to reject and refuse it.

❧

11. The goal being not away from us, but within ourselves, what we do then is to sense in ourselves the direction of Truth, that truth of which even a faint perception acts like a magnet or a scent, enabling us to follow an unseen trail out of the mazes of our experience.

❧

12. There is a point which we do not sufficiently seize—that God is not revealed to us by one avenue of truth alone, but by all the avenues of truth working together.

❧

13. Seeking truth is the first stage to-
wards finding it. After the seeking
comes the realization that Truth is
also seeking the Seeker himself.

∽

14. The truth of an idea is not a stagnant
property inherent in it. Truth happens
to an idea. It becomes true, is made
true by events. Its verity *is* in fact an
event, a process: the process namely of
its verifying itself, its veri-*fication*. Its
validity is the process of valid-*ation*.

∽

15. It is its own intrinsic content and
systematic wholeness which gives to
Truth all the certainty it can have.

∽

16. No pleasure is comparable to the standing upon the vantage ground of truth—a hill not to be commanded, and where the air is always clear and serene, and to see the error and wanderings and mists and tempests in the vale below.

༄

17. As long as we are not ever ready to sacrifice any given datum of rational science to an intuitive idea, science will always keep silent about absolute truth, or even about absolute knowledge which alone can explain the mechanics of our universe satisfactorily. Even the most exact science has always involved illogical magnitudes, such as zero and infinity.

༄

18. Truth, like an electron, is an organic unity of opposed parts.

๑

19. Eternal truth needs a human language that alters with the spirit of the times. The primordial images undergo ceaseless transformation and yet remain ever the same, but only in new form can they be understood anew. Always they require a new conception.

๑

20. Unless we ask with our whole being, heart and soul and mind, unless we can hardly eat or drink or sleep unless we know, unless life is no longer worth living without the experience

of living truth, we shall not gain it. We must desire truth more than life itself if we are to be worthy of experiencing it.

♋

21. We need to make a complete break with the world, which does not mean that we must outwardly do something to outrage it. But we must be prepared to think and act alone, loyal to the truth as we perceive it, seeking it for ourselves in every matter and not accepting it second-hand.

♋

22. Truth always lies just where we wish to escape. We must climb above the mountain of our suffering and of our

blindness, and everything that we have looked for with such longing will lie before us.

༄

23. What a person is, deep within himself, is the truth of his being, and what he does and seems to others must flow from that truth, be patterned upon it. Sincerity, the entire lack of duplicity, is at least an element in the search for Truth, which lies hidden within one's inmost self and does not take its rise in outer things.

༄

24. Aspire for the rest of the divine consciousness, but with a calm and deep aspiration. It can be ardent as

well as calm, but not impatient, restless or full of rajasic eagerness. Only in the quiet mind and being can the supramental Truth build its true creation.

❧

25. A doctrine or truth, presenting itself without proof on the bare value of its own nobility, is as disturbing a factor to the majority of men as would be the stranger without name or country. We are afraid of it; it is to us an invasion from an unknown world. And such it is; it is an invasion from another world, from the only real world, the world of Reality.

❧

26. There is a consciousness, or the potentiality of a consciousness, in man which unerringly hits the truth. It is incapable of giving rise to aught else than truth. That consciousness is free, but in its freedom does not deviate from the truth. In fact it is its absolute freedom from every imposition from without that makes it possible for it to express the truth, which is within itself.

ᕤᕤ

27. In a controversy, the instant we feel anger, we have already ceased striving for truth and have begun striving for ourselves.

ᕤᕤ

28. Essentially, Truth is an absolute and lies in an integrity of being. But it can be made to manifest only in forms of finiteness and relationship . . . . The discovery of the nature of Truth is in reality an uncovering of it.

∾

29. Truth is the spiritual white light which falls upon the prism of mankind and breaks into the many colours whereby individuals interpret it.

∾

30. When the mind is perfectly still and ceases to make images which are but

prejudice, distortion or preconception, when it has become a perfect mirror, neither convex nor concave, it will be able to reflect that truth which is the very nature of the Spirit. It will be able to create, move and function in the light of that truth.

༄

31. Living a life of truth does not consist merely in speaking the truth. To pretend to be what one is not is as corrupting as untruth in speech. There must be in one's heart a genuine love of truth.

April

DEVOTION

1. Speak each word, perform each action, face each situation before an inner altar where you kneel in uttermost adoration and self-surrender, under the seal and sign of your highest Self.

∽

2. O Spirit, I worship Thee as beauty and intelligence in the temple of Nature. I worship Thee as power in the temple of activity, and as peace in the temple of silence.

∽

3. Then shall thine Integrity and immortality be for nourishment,
With the Dominion of the Good Mind Devotion united with Righteousness shall increase endurance and power.

❧

4. All virtue is nothing other than an ordered and measured affection plainly directed to God for Himself alone.

❧

5. The offering up, the consecration, of physical, emotional, mental, or any other energy, on the Divine Altar—thus indeed is truly described the whole of Bhakti Yoga.

❧

6. Let each one create, after the pattern in his own heart, any image, figure of truth, or concept to which he can yield himself completely; he will then experience the rich effects of those cosmic influences which are ever showered from on high.

∿

7. And he who serveth Me exclusively by the Yoga of devotion, he, crossing beyond the qualities, he is fit to become the Eternal.

∿

8. O my God, since Thou art with me, and I must now, in obedience to Thy commands, apply mind to these outward things, I beseech Thee to grant

me the grace to continue in Thy Presence; and to this end do Thou prosper me with Thy assistance, receive all my works, and possess all my affections.

∞

9. He who is fully occupied in his desire for God has no time in this work to consider who is friend or foe, kin or stranger.

∞

10. Always a form is necessary for the growth of devotion. Hence it is necessary that, in order to realize that idea of the immanence of God, He must be worshipped in many forms, loved in many forms . . . . God shows

himself in many forms, so that He may attract the varying natures of men.

❧

11. I will mingle my inner devotional whispers with the prayers of all saints, and continuously offer them in the temples of silence and activity until I can' hear His whispers loudly, everywhere.

❧

12. All things in life lose their savor after the Heavenly Vision is seen, and nothing thenceforth is possible except to give utterly, holding back nothing, to an ideal of service, devotion, or renunciation.

❧

13. It is always the case that according to the character of the person's devotion will be the object to which he is devoted, call it by whatever name; essentially that object is what one makes it with his mind and heart.

∞

14. We have only to think strongly of an idea, and that which ensouls it or represents it will manifest itself to us. Any strong thought of devotion brings an instant response; the Universe would be dead if it did not.

∞

15. ... no devoted thing, that a man shall devote unto the Lord of all that he hath, both of man and beast; and of

the field of his possession, shall be sold or redeemed: every devoted thing is most holy unto the Lord.

❧

16. He who offereth to Me with devotion a leaf, a flower, a fruit, water, that I accept from the striving self, offered as it is with devotion.

❧

17. To turn all actions automatically into worship cannot be done by thought control only; there must be a strong aspiration in the heart which will bring about some realization of the feeling of the presence of the One to whom worship is offered. The bhakta

does not rely on his own effort alone, but on the grace and power of the Divine whom he adores.

❧

18. True devotion must expand one's entire being and expose it as the waters to the sun, so that the whole surface of one's nature is played upon by the actinic rays of Truth.

❧

19. Thou shalt love the Lord thy God with all thy heart, and with all thy soul, and with all thy mind . . . and thy neighbor as thyself.

❧

20. One-pointed devotion to the Supreme, a clear, well-balanced, intelligent development of the intellect and emotions, this is the road along which we must tread, if the Higher Consciousness is to be manifested on earth.

ॐ

21. To the man who is perfectly devoted inevitably will wisdom come and to him also right activity; for what should be his will in action save the will of the Lord he loves?

ॐ

22. The Perfect Man is a miniature of Reality; he is the microcosm, in

whom are reflected all the perfect attributes of the macrocosm.... Only the perfect Man knows God, loves God, and is lived by God.

ᐤᐤ

23. Whatsoever thou doest, whatsoever thou eatest, whatsoever thou offerest, whatsoever thou givest, whatsoever thou doest of austerity, ... do thou that as an offering unto Me.

ᐤᐤ

24. ... our sanctification [does] not depend upon *changing* our works, but in doing that for God's sake which commonly we do for our own.

ᐤᐤ

25. Devotion to a leader or a teacher, when it is pure, is always to that which is true, beautiful, and good in him. Devotion to an ideal is to the measure of Truth which is embodied in the conception of that idea.

∽

26. Receive no other thought of Him, even not all of these unless you desire to have them. For a naked intent directed to God without any further cause than Himself fully suffices.

∽

27. Because you are truly this, O Wise One with light and Good Mind, Give me this sign: the entire remaking of this existence

That a greater joy may be mine in
your worship and praise.

∞

28. Lift up your heart to Him even at
your meals and when you are in
company; the least little remembrance
will always be acceptable to Him.
You need not cry very loud; He is
nearer to us than we think.

∞

29. He who doeth actions for Me, whose
supreme good I am, My devotee,
freed from attachment without hatred
of any being, he cometh unto Me . . .

∞

30. One thing I tell you—that a pure intention of love unto God for Himself alone ... is more profitable to the health of your soul, more worthy in itself, and more pleasing to God and all His holy creatures now and forever more ... than if the eye of your soul were opened in contemplation so that you had a vision of all the angels and saints in God's Presence, or heard the joy and the very melody of their praise.

May

INTUITION

1. The word "complete" signifies the quality of pure intuition. In difficult circumstances, where there is a discord of considerations and confusion in the act of weighing and balancing them, the way to determine the best course of action is not through calculation, not through such weighing and balancing, but through that center of gravity within ourselves which will move us along the line of right and perfect action.

∽

2. Intuition is coming "face to face," a beholding. The mind proceeds stage by stage to a result; the intuition perceives the result instantly. The mind remembers. The intuition has no need to remember because it is perceiving.

༅

3. By direct perception we feel the presence of *mind*; by intellectual circumlocution we arrive at the notion that thought is a dance of molecules in the brain. Is there any doubt that intuition here beholds more truly the heart of life?

༅

4. If you only think of it for a moment, none of the things worth having are subject to proof. The moment you begin to try to prove them they seem to fall to pieces. Doubts arise on all sides, and your faith is in danger of being wrecked; faith, I mean, in anything that you value. To know intuitively is really to take the "pairs of opposites" and, transcending them on a higher plane, resolve or synthesize them there.

∼

5. Reason is the clumsy weapon of the scientists—intuition the unerring guide of the seer.

∼

6. As rivers run into the deep and lose name and form and disappear, so comes, from name and form released, the wise man to the Deity. The Deity, therefore, we will take to be the intuition. The rivers are the processes of mind, or emotion; and as those rivers become deeper and stronger and truer, so they lose name and form and as it were disappear.

✺

7. Human life is the allegory of the spirit, a drama of the unfoldment of consciousness; and the emancipation of woman in the world corresponds to and symbolizes the emergence of the intuition in the consciousness.

✺

8. In the intuition there is a flash of
   direct knowledge, but now the great
   structure of the intellect has been
   built up through intervening ages and
   by its means the intuitive knowledge
   can descend to our daily life in full
   consciousness. Without that structure,
   without the intellect as instrument,
   the thinker within would not be able
   to interpret his vision in intelligible
   language to his fellow-men; the artist
   may be ever so great but he needs an
   instrument to play on.

ᄽ

9. One in whom persuasion and belief
   Had ripened into faith, and faith
       become
   A passionate intuition.

ᄽ

10. It is possible, through the faculty of Intuition or Buddhi, to create things which are entirely new, for when the faculty is developed it creates centers in the consciousness from which there emerge ideas that are new and true, and because they are true, also beautiful.

༖

11. The only authority you recognize, the only command you allow, must be the Voice of that Intuition which is unalterable, which nothing in the world can shake.

༖

12. Intuitive knowledge ... is free from any partiality or dualism, it has

overcome the extremes of emphasizing subject or object, it is the synthetic vision of the world, the experience of cosmic consciousness, in which the Infinite is not only conceptualized but realized.

❧

13. Mankind is constantly being taught in this world in two manners—through tuition and intuition. The statement is true in a general way, but the root of the matter is that a man really *understands* only through intuition.

❧

14. Intuition . . . tends to have a universalizing effect. It takes you out of particulars into universals, out of

circumstances into the force which is at work bringing about those circumstances. It is, in other words, a partial introduction into the one life which emanates from the whole nature.

∽

15. Our secret creative will divines its counterpart in others, experiencing its own universality, and this intuition builds a road toward knowledge of the power which is itself a spark within us.

∽

16. It was never the intention of the Occultists really to conceal what they had been writing from the earnest determined students, but rather to

lock up their information for safety's sake, in a secure safe box, the key to which is intuition.

❧

17. Knowledge has three degrees—opinion, science, illumination. The means or instrument of the first is sense; of the second, dialectic; of the third, intuition. To the last I subordinate reason. It is absolute knowledge founded on the identity of the mind knowing with the object known.

❧

18. Go into the silent places of your heart; enter into the chambers so quiet and still, of your inner being. . . . Intuition

will then come to you. You will have knowledge immediately; you will know truth instantly.

～

19. Where reason cannot think out the right solution of a perplexity, intuition can step triumphantly forward with an immediate presentation of it. Reasoning is self-conscious, active and inquisitive, whereas intuition is spontaneous, receptive, and passive. An intuition need have no logical connection with former thinking. Hence it may open up an entirely new horizon on that particular subject.

～

20. Intuition leaves no footmarks. The movement arises within the soul, possesses it possibly to intoxication, and passes away. It has not been summoned, and it cannot be retained by any act of will. . . . What is characteristic of intuition is not the absence of the conditions of a new experience, but the fullness of their presence and the intense fusion of their functions.

ᔄ

21. We must not belittle the mind. It is one of the most wonderful powers that any individual may possess. But the intuition can do two things for us which the mind cannot do. First, it can bring into simple formulae that which the mind has found out either in this life or in past lives. Second,

intuition can intimate the future, that which is to be.

❦

22. Use your will power, and may the benediction of Truth, and the Divine Presence of Him the Inscrutable be upon thee and help thee to open thy intuition.

❦

23. What we need to overcome is our unfounded suspicion of the intuition as the stranger from nowhere; we must begin to realize, especially in philosophy, that all man has ever thought of any worth in the history of philosophy, he has been taught as the result of that inner and direct

awareness of truth which we call
intuition and not as the prodigious
result of wearisome reasoning.

❧

24. The quality, nature, life, essence of a
thing—be it metal, a tree, a grain of
wood, a painting, an animal, a human
being—can be felt subjectively only
with that higher faculty which we can
only call Intuition, a form of direct
knowledge.

❧

25. The conqueror and king in each one
of us is the intuition, the knower of
truth, of the life, and the future. Let
that knower awaken in us and drive
the horses of the mind, emotions, and

physical body on the pathway which that king has chosen.

◦◦

26. The truth is that till the neophyte attains to the condition necessary for that degree of Illumination to which, and for which, he is entitled and fitted, most if not all of the Secrets are incommunicable. . . . The illumination must come from within.

◦◦

27. The idea that consciousness exists in all persons is an intuition. With the means at his disposal the scientist cannot prove scientifically that consciousness exists in any other person than himself. The realm above con-

scious mind is the world of arche-
types in the older philosophies.

ॐ

28. The intuition is a kind of bridge
between the future and the present.
It is a larger consciousness not yet
developed or fulfilled, any more than
the consciousness of mind or emotions
is perfected and fulfilled: but it is
larger consciousness, giving us a far
larger horizon. It takes us into a far
kingdom of nature ... in which we
feel extraordinarily at home.

ॐ

29. It is just in these rare silences of our
busy lives that the intuition can speak
to us; it is only when the illusion-

bound intellect with its noisy self-assertion is quiet for a while that the voice of living truth can be heard. The moment of illumination may well be the outcome of years of mental search calling forth, as it were, by induction a corresponding activity in the world of the Real, where the untrammeled mind sees the vision and speaks to the mind in prison. But it is always the flash of intuition that shows us the truth and coordinates our laboriously gathered intellectual material.

❧

30. That ideal of perfection . . . the aspirant makes for himself as perfect as he is able to conceive it, knowing all the time that his most perfect

dreaming is but the faintest shadow of the reality whence this reflection has come.

৵

31. [There is] a Divine Intuition which needs no teachers from without. It is not conjecture, hunch, or wishful thinking. It is a faculty which speaks only the language of truth. All falsehood has been eliminated from the nature of the man who is able to exercise it all the time.

June

BEAUTY

1. The creation of ideal beauty in a form, whether of thought, words, music, sculpture, painting, architecture, or dance, has this effect: it touches in the beholders or listeners . . . those centers of consciousness which are receptive to the idea reflected in the form, and thus helps the consciousness to be active on a plane nearer to reality.

༄

2. Let us seek to fulfill the beautiful in ourselves, that which is the beautiful for us at our present level of growth.

Let us live in every detail of our lives as beautifully as we know how.

∽

3. Beauty is a pledge of the possible conformity between the soul and nature, and consequently a ground of faith in the supremacy of the good.

∽

4. Beauty is something both within and beyond us—within, so far as we surely know it when we see it; beyond, because we feel that every item of beauty is a symbol or an instance of some deeper, more permanent beauty we can never grasp. As much as anything, beauty is the divine play.

∽

5. Beauty is a form of Genius—is higher, indeed, than Genius, as it needs no explanation.

෨

6. An idea is perceived as beautiful because it embodies a law. In its lawfulness lies the esssence of its beauty . . . . When we are affected by that law or by some of the laws, which are in the beautiful thing, we say it is beautiful.

෨

7. Beauty is the repose of perfect action in sound or color or form, and well has it been said that of all things in the material world art alone endures.

෨

8. For the world is not painted or adorned, but is from the beginning beautiful; and God has not made some beautiful things, but Beauty is the creator of the universe.

❧

9. What is the magic of the conjuring harmony in music that suddenly blinds our eyes? What is the sovereign gesture in the plastic arts? In other words, what inevitable revelation is there in beauty that tells us authoritatively that this is truth, and makes our assent reverberate in a thrill of grateful recognition?

❧

10. As knowledge feeds the mind, so beauty nourishes the heart. The intellect survives upon its uncertainties; the emotions, upon their acceptances. In a strange way thoughts are negative and feelings positive. The mind demands; the heart gives . . . . It responds instinctively to the invitation of beauty.

∽

11. When a beautiful soul harmonizes with a beautiful form, and the two are cast in one mould, that will be the fairest of sights to him who has the eye to contemplate the vision.

∽

12. For beauty is not a matter of the conventions of men or of Gods; a thing is beautiful only because it follows the sole law of beauty—that it shall be a mirror of an Archetype. Hence a beautiful rose is beautiful not because of its symmetry or color or rhythm, but only because its "accidents" of symmetry, color, and rhythm mirror an archetypal Rose. A beautiful face, or hand, or foot, or any member, is beautiful because, to one sensitive to beauty, each is a window through which he glimpses an Archetype, a Masterpiece of the Artist of artists.

∽

13. There is an abiding beauty which may be appreciated by those who will see

things as they are and who will ask
for no reward except to see. There is
a high aesthetic pleasure in seeing the
truth clear-eyed and in not being
afraid of things.

∾

14. . . , beauty is life when life unveils her
holy face.
But you are life and you are the veil.
Beauty is eternity gazing at itself in a
mirror.
But you are eternity and you are the
mirror.

∾

15. There seems to be no way of ana-
lyzing it that satisfactorily explains
the direct impact beauty itself has

upon us and the certainty with which we recognize it. The explanation of beauty really rests in our recognition of it.

∞

16. You cannot see beauty outside unless you have beauty within you. You cannot understand beauty unless you yourself are beautiful inside.

∞

17. Beauty is a pledge of the possible conformity between the soul and nature, and consequently a ground of faith in the supremacy of good.

∞

18. Is not beauty created at every en-
counter between a man and life, in
which he repays his debt by focusing
on the living moment all the power
which life has given him as an
obligation? Beauty—for the one who
pays his debt. For others, too,
perhaps.

19. If you develop your sense of Brotherhood, you will become more sensitive
to Beauty; if you will learn to create
Beauty, you will instinctively feel a
sense of comradeship with all that
lives.

20. Beauty is indefinable because it is an expression of Life . . . . Life ever seeks to integrate. When that integration is complete there is beauty.

൨

21. Beauty is the vestment and expression of the Creator; He made the pursuit of the Beautiful the Supreme Law of the Universe; every insect, shrub, and even crystal, senses and obeys that law and makes itself and environment beautiful.

൨

22. Though we travel the world over to find the beautiful we must carry it with us, or we find it not. The best of beauty is a finer charm than skill in surfaces, in outlines, or rules of art

can ever teach, namely a radiation from the work of art, of human character—a wonderful expression through stone, or canvas, or musical sound, of the deepest and simplest attributes of our nature, and therefore most intelligible at last to those souls which have these attributes.

∽

23. The Path is not hard, if you would only look and choose the right road; admire, but do not criticize; sympathize, but do not condemn. And you who long for the Good, the True, and the Beautiful shall not need to travel far to find the Beautiful, for you shall then realize that you are the Beautiful in yourselves.

∽

24. Whatever is in any way beautiful hath its source of beauty in itself, and is complete in itself; praise forms no part of it. So it is none the worse nor the better for being praised.

❧

25. There will be always one or two who hold
    Earth's coin of less account than fairy gold;
    Their Treasurer, not the spoil of crowns and kings,
    But the dim beauty at the heart of things.

❧

26. There is beauty, whether in Nature or art, where there is an expression of a

fragment of Divine thought, when it embodies a ray of the Divine Nature. That nature is also in the consciousness of man, who is an individual focus of the universal life.

༄

27. Beauty comes as something gratituitously generous. It is benevolent redundancy, having a value that is quite different from mere utility . . . . Its purpose seems to be to enrich and not merely to preserve life, and its appeal is to reason. It is thus difficult to conceive of beauty as proceeding from an unintelligent source.

༄

28. There is no such thing as relative beauty; Beauty is *absolute,* at least as absolute as anything on this earth can be. It is taste, or the appreciation of beauty which is relative.

∽

29. For who can doubt, really, that a view of the universe not restricted by our human limitations, would disclose that reality as it is intimated to us through truth, beauty, and goodness— through art, science and religion— would turn out to be a unity far more perfect than we can imagine. and far more beauitful?

∽

30. There is a deep purpose in Nature, which is the self-unfoldment of all things, of the hidden nature in them. In this unfoldment there is joy, there is creation, there is beauty.

July

COURAGE

1. Do not be afraid of your difficulties, do not wish you could be in other circumstances than you are, for when you have made the best of an adversity it becomes the stepping-stone to a splendid opportunity.

❧

2. Courage in strife is common enough; even the dogs have it. But the courage which can face the ultimate defeat of a life of good will . . . that is different, that is victory.

❧

3. The brave man is the humble and true man whose faith in Life and its increasing purpose is like that of the little bird who flies undoubtingly into the empyrean.

∞

4. The type of courage which is induced in oneself by self-suggestion or by putting on an exaggeratedly brave front is really a mask of fear. Because you are afraid at heart, you put on an air which suggests the opposite of fear. Such so-called courage does not last long.

∞

5. No soul that aspires can ever fail to rise; no heart that loves can ever be

abandoned. Difficulties exist only that in overcoming them we may grow strong, and they only who have suffered are able to save.

❧

6. There is a . . . road, steep and thorny, difficult to follow, but which the Great Ones of the human race have trodden. It is the quick road, but the difficult one. It is the road of self-conquest, the road of the giving up of self for the All.

❧

7. It is the broad view and the long vision which alone can cure our fearfulness and fortify our steps. A

longer vista lies before us than even anthropology can offer of the past.

❧

8. There is only one way ... to know what one knows; and that is to risk one's convictions in an act, to commit them in a responsibility ... one does not know what one knows, or even what one wishes to know, until one is challenged, and must lay down a stake.

❧

9. To resist, to survive, to win through is the end to which the life principle sets itself with such singleness of aim as to unfold a wealth of potentiality astounding to us in looking backward.

❧

10. One who has not the courage to face patiently and firmly life and its difficulties will never be able to go through the still greater inner difficulties of the sadhana. The very first lesson in this Yoga is to face life and its trials with a quiet mind, a firm courage, and an entire reliance on the Divine Shakti.

๛

11. The most decisive battles of the world are fought not on external battlefields, but in the consciences of men. No man can extemporize character. In every realm life does ambush us. We must be ready beforehand.

๛

12. It is only by grasping this nettle, danger, that we pluck this flower, safety; those who flee from emotion, from intimacy, from the shocks and perils attendant upon all close human relationships, end in being attacked by unseen Furies in the ultimate stronghold of their spirit.

༖

13. As a Master of the Wisdom once put it, courage belongs to the immortal soul. The mortal body knows only the law of self-preservation. Courage is the red badge of our immortal Spirit, who lives and grows by sacrifice and faith and love.

༖

14. The citadel is within all men and women of good will. To find it is an individual quest—the most urgent, significant quest of our lives....We can march out of our invulnerable selves, all banners flying, and take risks, seize opportunity with strong hands, meet change with willing adaptability. We shall be often hurt...but in a real, abiding sense we shall be safe.

∽

15. And indeed the worst, the most horrible reality, has always a compensation at the heart of it, if only one can look at it steadily.

∽

16. Never forget that Life can only be nobly inspired and rightly lived if you take it bravely and gallantly, as a splendid adventure in which you are setting out into an unknown country, to face many a danger, to meet many a joy, to find many a comrade, to win and lose many a battle.

∽

17. Is there somewhere, in the stuff that holds humanity together, some force, some conservation of spiritual energy that saves the very core of every noble hope and gathers all men's visions some day, some way, into the reality of progress?

∽

18. There needs not a great soul to make a hero; there needs a God-created soul which will be true to its origin; that will be a great soul!

∞

19. When some occasional test, dismay, or self-pity took hold of me, I formed a habit of saying to myself, "This is your special stunt. It's up to you to do this thing just as if you had all the facilities. Go at it boldly and you'll find unexpected forces closing round you and coming to your aid."

∞

20. Much stress is laid upon the necessity of courage in all systems of occult

training. If a man enters upon the Path he will have to face misrepresentation, calumny, and misunderstanding.

᧞

21. Never measure the height of a mountain until you have reached the top. Then you will see how low it was.

᧞

22. The dawn dares when it breaks. To attempt, to brave, persist and persevere, to be faithful to one's self, to wrestle with destiny, to astound the catastrophe by the slight fear which it causes us . . . to hold firm and withstand—such is the example which

people need and which electrifies them.

❧

23. We must accept life for what it actually is—a challenge to our quality without which we should never know of what stuff we are made, or grow to our full stature.

❧

24. Actual physical courage is needed, too. There are many dangers and difficulties on the Path not by any means symbolical, or on higher planes only; tests of bravery and endurance do come to us in the course of our progress, and we must be prepared for them.

❧

25. Fire burns our fingers and the action of our hearts prevents our running up mountainsides; but only the gods have put a veto on the adventures of our minds.

❧

26. The fourth jewel is Endurance, that strong power which can bear without giving way, which can face all things in the search for truth, and never fall back because of difficulty or of peril.

❧

27. The more decisions you are forced to make alone, the more you are aware of your freedom to choose. I hold that we cannot be said to be aware of our minds save under responsibility.

❧

28. You are not alone; the centuries fight for you; eternity is your ally; you are in the keeping of the One who holds you with love that will not let you go.

❧

29. We form a habit of conquering as insistent as any other habit. Victory becomes, to some degree, a state of mind. Knowing ourselves superior to the anxieties, troubles, and worries which obsess us, we *are* superior to them. It is a question of attitude in confronting them.

❧

30. ... if sorrow that you shrink from comes upon you, remember that the

hand of love allows it thus to fall, and that in bearing that sorrow bravely, you are swiftly working out your own deliverance.

∼

31. To live intelligently, man must have that buoyancy of spirit, call it courage, and willingness to accept any and every state that may confront him, which alone will enable him to live without burdens, a free man in the true sense of the term.

HUMILITY

1. Humility bespeaks the proximity of greatness, the near event of the emptying of the waters of oneself into the ocean to which they belong.

∾

2. Do not scrupulously confine yourself to fixed rules, or particular forms of devotion, but act with faith in God, with love and humility.

3. Humility is perfect quietness of the heart. It is for me never to be fretted,

vexed, irritated, sore, or disappointed. It is to be at rest when nobody praises me and when I am blamed or despised. It is to have a blessed home in the Lord, where I can go and shut the door and kneel and talk to my Father in secret, and where I am at peace as in a deep sea of calmness when all around and above me is troubled.

∾

4. The true heart wears always the veil of modesty . . . you can see all the while the golden outlines and, by that token, you know that it is glowing and burning with a pure and steady flame.

∾

5. What doth the Lord require of thee, but to do justly, and to love mercy, and to walk humbly with thy God?

෴

6. Be utterly humble and you shall hold to the foundation of peace.

෴

7. The wisest poet keeps something of the vision of a child. Though he may think a thousand things that a child could not understand, he is always a beginner, close to the original meanings of life.

෴

8. Except in faith, nobody is humble. The mask of weakness or of phariseeism is not the naked face of humility.

And, except in faith, nobody is proud. The vanity displayed in all its varieties by the spiritually immature is not pride.

To be, in faith, both humble and proud: that is, to live, to know that in God I am nothing, but that God is in me.

∾

9. Where there is charity and wisdom, there is neither fear nor ignorance. Where there is patience and humility, there is neither anger nor vexation.

∾

10. I walk before God in simple faith, with humility and with love, and I apply myself diligently to do nothing and think nothing which may displease Him. I hope that when I have done what I can, He will do with me what He pleases.

❧

11. Humility is not mere consciousness of our littlenesses, which might be only a feeling of disappointment at not being as important as we would wish to be, nor is it self-depreciation. Rather is it the eradication of all self-conceit, so we become sweet and beautiful, have an openness of mind and heart, and feel a really deep respect for another, whoever he may be, based on the recognition of his Godhead.

❧

12. Humility, that low, sweet root
    From which all heavenly virtues
    shoot.

❧

13. Whosoever shall exalt himself shall be
    abased, and he that shall humble
    himself shall be exalted.

❧

14. Nothing will sustain you more
    potently than the power to recognize
    in your humdrum routine, as perhaps
    it may be thought, the true poetry of
    life—the poetry of the commonplace,
    of the ordinary man, of the plain,
    toilworn woman, with their loves and
    their joys, their sorrows and their griefs.

❧

15. True humility, the highest virtue, mother of them all.

꙳

16. It is a mistake to think that service of a humble character is not of importance. It is the attitude of the server which is most important.

꙳

17. Humility is to make a right estimate of one's self. It is no humility for a man to think less of himself than he ought, though it might rather puzzle him to do that.

꙳

18. To reach perfection, we must all pass, one by one, through the death of self-effacement. And, on this side of it . . . never find the way to anyone who has passed through it.

❧

19. Humility does not consist in professing or bemoaning one's insignificance. *The Voice of the Silence* says: "Be humble if wisdom thou wouldst attain." Humility is a necessary qualification, for without it, it is not possible for a man to be really wise.

❧

20. Humility, a sense of reverence before the sons of heaven—of all the prizes

that a mortal man might win, these, I
say are wisest; these are best.

∽

21. The only wisdom we can hope to
    acquire
    Is the wisdom of humility; humility is
    endless.

∽

22. You must become as aware of in-
    significance as you think you are
    of significance; not seek feelings
    of significance alone.
    The humble are so because they must
    be so; and worst of all men or
    women are those who practice
    humility for the purpose of
    pride . . .

∽

23. The higher we are placed, the more
humbly we should walk.

❦

24. And if a lowly singer dries one tear,
Or soothes one humble human heart
in pain,
Be sure his homely verse to God is
dear,
And not one stanza has been sung in
vain.

❦

25. The pride of the cup is in the drink,
its humility in the serving. What,
then, do its defects matter?

❦

26. The tumult and the shouting dies;
    The captains and the kings depart;
    Still stands Thine ancient sacrifice,
    An humble and a contrite heart.

ॐ

27. In all religions humility is regarded as
    a fundamental virtue. It is not a
    secondary requirement, but basic. If a
    person has the quality of humility,
    and along with it the alertness, the
    blend would bring about the right
    temper in himself.

ॐ

28. Humility is the abasement of the
    heart to Him who knoweth the
    unseen. The perfection of the re-

collection of God is contemplation,
and the perfection of humility is
being well pleased with God.

ᠬᠥ

29. Humility before the flower at the
timber line is the gate which gives
access to the path up the open fell.

ᠬᠥ

30. Humility is the most difficult of all
virtues to achieve; nothing dies harder
than the desire to think well of
oneself.

ᠬᠥ

31. True humility becomes the source of
our wisdom; the more a man knows,

the more he realizes how little he knows, and the most wise is the most humble.

September

THE ART OF LIVING

1. Anyone who sets out to master the art of living . . . cannot but discover how difficult it is . . . . The vital questions to be put to ourselves in each and every situation are: What should be the nature of our approach to it; what the nature of our thoughts and feelings therein; what action shall we perform? In the mass of circumstances which beset us on every side, what is the direction of true progress?

᠙

2. First, Life's great decisions must be correct decisions and life's great

choices, wise choices. Second, one must be prepared and willing to pay the full price of weariness, disappointment, opposition, and if need be, defeat, in fulfillment of the purpose to which life has been dedicated. Third, since such demands as these overpass the natural powers of unaided flesh and blood, one must learn the art and establish the habit of tapping those heavenly reservoirs of wisdom and strength which are lavishly offered to faith and are available for human help.

∽

3. The strings of our daily life are few in number, but we can make endless melody thereon.

∽

4. The art of integrated living consists in the spirit of intelligent cooperation between nature and spirit. Nature is blind without spirit; spirit is lame without nature ... nature and spirit— by virtue of their purposive togetherness—can make life gloriously meaningful.

❧

5. Everything that *is* is an opportunity of the percipient eye and the understanding heart to learn, which means to grow; and when you realize that suffering and pain are two of the means by which we grow, then come peace in the heart and rest to the mind.

❧

6. Having done your best, decide; and when you have decided, act; for you have done all you can. Then watch the results; see what is the outcome of your decision; and you will discover by that outcome whether you judged rightly or wrongly. If you judge wrongly, do not regret. You did your best, and you have gained a new experience by the blunder, and it will help you in the future.

∂

7. For "living" does not mean that we enjoy the world till all passion is spent, but rather that we stand at the helm and know that we are masters of our fate and not its slave—master of our joys and master of our sorrows. For wherever there is joy,

there will be sorrow also. It is up to us, and it lies within us. We have only to find the path.

∾

8. You cannot have the thing you will not give away. You cannot be free of the thing you hold. To hold on is to belong to the thing held, a bond. What you set free belongs to you. You do not belong to it, for you belong to love . . . . To belong to love is to have life and life abundantly, for then life belongs to you.

∾

9. The first creation in the process of self-realization, which is the discovery of the hidden Truth, is the creation

or recreation of ourselves as a vessel of Truth. "Ourselves" means our living, our every thought and action. We have to mould all of it and every part nearer to the goal of our aspiration. And this is a work of art, the greatest of all existing arts.

∽

10. Only a life lived for others is a life worth while. The man who regards his own life and that of his fellow creatures as meaningless is not merely unhappy but hardly fit for life. Try not to become a man of success, but rather try to become a man of value.

∽

11. Let us sit down quietly and realize that no event in life is unjust, but somewhere from the long past our ancient "sin" has found us out; that every event is remedial, and that it has a message, a lesson for us.

∼

12. Truly, we cannot arrange our lives wisely unless we know the meaning of life; we shall but continue to seek our riches where no riches are, to waste our energies where they do but harm, forgetting all the while the wisdom of Ruskin's saying: "There is no wealth but life."

∼

13. Finally, brethren, whatsoever things are true, whatsoever things are honest, whatsoever things are just, whatsoever things are pure, whatsoever things are lovely, whatsoever things are of good report; if there be any virtue, and if there be any praise, think on these things.

&

14. Not out of right practice comes right thinking, but out of right thinking comes right practice. It matters enormously what you think. If you think falsely, you will act mistakenly; if you think basely, your conduct will suit your thinking.

&

15. If man talks much about the Teaching but acts not in accordance therewith, he is but little better than the cowherd who only counts the cattle of others. He is no disciple of the Blessed One. If a man talks little about the Teaching but puts its precepts into practice, ridding himself of craving and of hatred and of delusion, possessed of right knowledge, truly delivered in mind, cleaving to nothing in this or in any other world—he is a disciple of the Blessed One.

ॐ

16. Taking up your cross is carrying whatever you find is given you to carry as well and stoutly as you can without making faces or calling

people to come and look at you. All you have to do is to keep your back straight and not think of what is on it—above all do not *boast* of what is on it.

෴

17. Live every moment as though you were building a temple.

෴

18. You carve your own destiny; you make yourself what you are; what you are now is precisely what in past lives you have made yourself now to be; and what you will in the future be, you are now making yourself to become.

෴

19. One cannot conquer the evil in himself by resisting it, but . . . by transmuting its energies into other forms. The energy that expresses itself in the form of evil is the same energy which expresses itself in the form of good; and thus the one may be transmuted into the other.

～

20. In the ordinary course of our life we can observe that spiritual development does not so much consist in the *solution* of our problems, as in growing *beyond* them.

～

21. To every man comes a time when he must face himself . . . . To learn the

art of confronting ourselves before it is too late—and to do this every day—is to discover a source of strength as wonderful as it is accessible.

❧

22. Life is truly an *education,* which word does not mean putting or cramming something into a child's head which was not there before, but gently and patiently "leading out" into expression latent and undeveloped power.

❧

23. You have to learn to distinguish in everything around you, and in every one around you, between the perma-

nent element and the impermanent, between the surface and the content, as it were, between the eternal and the transitory.

❧

24. Reason is not an end in itself but a tool for the individual to use in adjusting himself to the values and purposes of living which are beyond reason. Just as the teeth are intended to chew *with*, not to chew themselves, so the mind is intended to think *with*, not to worry about. It is an instrument to live with, not to live for.

❧

25. But one thing is certain: unconscious-
ness or wanting to remain unconscious,
to escape the call to development and
avoid the venture of life, is sin. For
though growing old is the inescapable
lot of all creatures, growing old meaningfully is a task ordained for man
alone.

26. God does not die on the day when
we cease to believe in a personal
deity, but we die on the day when
our lives cease to be illuminated by
the steady radiance, renewed daily, of
a wonder, the source of which is
beyond all reason.

27. The mystery of life as a state of being on earth can never be solved so long as it is studied separately and apart from Universal Life.

✧

28. Emotional balance and maturity are essential ingredients of self-development. To this end one has to get closely acquainted with oneself. One has to be aware of the fundamental drives and desires of one's nature and fulfill them in an intelligent and organized fashion. One has to learn to relate to others meaningfully.

✧

29. Every individual must himself tread the path of realization, for only the

knowledge that is won by experience has living, i.e., life-giving value.

സ

30. There is a way of living so vitally, freshly, originally, spontaneously and dynamically that life becomes a transformation, a state of perpetual joy, a native ecstasy which nothing can take away.

October

HARMONY

1. There must be harmony, and not merely the kind of order which ensures stability by keeping together the individual disparate elements. Harmony is a strange subjective fact of creation which can only be felt or experienced. It is the foundation of beauty.

༖

2. All pain and suffering are results of want of Harmony, and . . . the one terrible and only cause of the disturbance of Harmony is selfishness in some form or another.

༖

3. I do not know what love is. I gather examples of its workability. I know it has a practical utility, as well as a spiritual glory. I know it never fails to change the thing it touches. Out of disorder it brings order, out of chaos, harmony.

❧

4. Each one is a theme in the Divine Harmony, though we are in different stages of unfoldment of that theme.

❧

5. Where the heart is full of kindness which seeks no injury to another, either in act or thought or wish, this full love creates an atmosphere of harmony, whose benign power touches

with healing all who come within its influence. Peace in the heart radiates peace to other hearts, even more surely than contention breeds contention.

❧

6. Yoga is literally union, and it means harmony with the Divine Law, the becoming one with the divine life, by the subduing of all outward-going energies. To reach this, balance must be gained, equilibrium, so that the self . . . shall not be affected by pleasure or pain, desire or aversion.

❧

7. The most perfect harmony is really an absolute unity where the action of every part is so joined with that of

every other that the total effect is simple and unique, like a perfect chord.

❧

8. To be in harmony with the life principle and the conquest principle is to be in harmony with power; and to be in harmony with power is to be strong as a matter of course.

❧

9. When a man acts harmoniously, he acts in accordance with the universal scheme and law; and harmony in consciousness and thought, and therefore in action, is what men understand by the term ethics which are

based on the very structural harmony of the Universe.

❧

10. Wherever life is, there is the process of building; different elements are brought together into relations which make of them a living whole, capable of functioning together in harmony.

❧

11. The note, A natural, is in itself insignificant. But the note A natural, when combined in a certain way with a certain number of other notes, becomes an essential part of the "Hymn to Joy" in Beethoven's Choral Symphony. It is conceivable

that the moment of world existence of which we are each aware during a human lifetime may be an essential part of a musical whole that is yet to be unfolded.

❧

12. Our principles are the Seven-Stringed Lyre of Apollo, truly . . . the Occultist who knows how to tighten them and tune his violin in harmony with the vibrations of color and sound, will extract divine harmony from them.

❧

13. The peace that arises from the very mode of one's life and action and does not turn into boredom is not static, a condition, like that of a

stagnant pool, which has no means of cleansing itself, but a deep feeling that springs from within and permeates one's whole being, in the very midst of movements so harmonized that there is no break in the harmony and unity of that being.

∾

14. Beauty of style and harmony and grace and good rhythm depend on simplicity.

∾

15. As the Soul feels itself growing too strong to be shaken, and yet feels every thrill that comes from without, it has a sense of wider life, it has a sense of fuller harmony, it has a sense

of every-increasing consciousness, of ever-growing oneness with that of which it is part.

❧

16. Harmony is the law of life, discord its shadow, whence springs suffering, the teacher, the awakener of consciousness.

❧

17. Perfect harmony is perfect balance, and the true aspirant is he who balances the necessary qualities in himself, in whom there is not the unbalance of an exaggeration nor faltering from an essential principle.

❧

18. . . . the very heart of Nature is harmony, the very fabric and structure of the Universe is co-ordination and co-operation, spiritual union.

❧

19. Through joy and sorrow, and pain and pleasure, the soul comes to a knowledge of itself; then begins the task of learning the laws of life, that the discords may be resolved and the harmony restored.

❧

20. The consciousness that is completely open to any form of harmony, whether in sound, color, thought, or anything else, is thereby unified and

integrated; it becomes charged with the quality pervading that form.

❧

21. Truth is harmony. It is that unified whole of existence in which all apparent contradictions are reconciled. It is also that self-coherent vision of existence in which all fragmentary viewpoints are harmonized.

❧

22. Moderation is therefore the keynote . . . and the harmonizing of all the constituents in man, till they vibrate in perfect attunement with the One, the Supreme Self.

❧

23. The endeavor of Nature through man, and of man as he learns his identity with her, is to create an order of harmony and beauty out of the material that comes into human life and is meant for human use.

❧

24. All Action, on every plane, produces disturbance in the balanced harmony of the Universe ... harmony can only be restored by the reconverging *to the same point* of the forces which were set in motion from it.

❧

25. Harmony dwells in self-control. It brings the two poles of existence into union with each other. It turns all

opposites into complementaries. It is the means of giving oneself to those around oneself. It consitutes the essence of yoga, and makes one's whole being a perfect channel through which all that one is in Eternity may flow forth into one's time manifestation.

❧

26. The fullest measure of happiness can be attained in life only by following the law of balanced distribution. Balanced distribution is an operative principle of the concept of harmony. It overrules all species of extremism and one-sided exaggeration. It organizes the different drives of personality in a balanced whole.

❧

27. It is only through observing the law of harmony that individual life hereafter can be obtained; and the farther the inner and outer man deviate from this fount of harmony, whose source lies in our divine spirit, the more difficult it is to regain ground.

৩

28. Harmony is unity in diversity.

৩

29. Harmony in the physical and mathematical world of sense, is *justice* in the spiritual one. Justice produces harmony, and injustice discord; and discord, on a cosmical scale, means chaos—annihilation.

৩

30. So in harmonious living one has to take into account all the fundamental urges and aspirations of life. Life well lived is vital energy intelligently distributed among the various urges of life.

ॐ

31. A rhythmic harmony in oneself and an outward-turned sensitiveness is the foundation for yoga, in which there is union between knower and known in a state of harmony comprehending both.

November

UNDERSTANDING

1. The first Law of Understanding is that in general the same hopes, sorrows, joys, troubles, fears, encompass us all. The same Destiny beckons us. The same Love enfolds us. The same Justice educates us.

෨

2. The second Law of Understanding is that each living creature—superhuman, human, subhuman—through his own individual circumstances of personality in terms of physical, emotional, mental and higher consciousness, in terms of his nationality, in terms of his faith, in

terms of his race, in terms of his environment, is unfolding his being to its perfection.

❧

3. The third law of understanding is that difference does not normally imply superiority and inferiority—be such difference what it may.

❧

4. The fourth law of understanding is that misunderstanding retards growth, while understanding accelerates growth —be the growth in terms of individuality or of collectivity.

❧

5. The fifth law of understanding is that everywhere the available best is happening, and if a better is not happening, it is because the world . . . is still unable to achieve it.

❧

6. The sixth law of understanding is that the available best is but a temporary halting place on the way to a better.

❧

7. The seventh law of understanding is that Love and Justice rule the world and are expressed in the preceding six laws.

❧

8. There can be no right action without understanding. The essence of all understanding lies in experiencing the very being of the object to be understood.

❧

9. Reason is weak, when measured against its never-ending task. Weak, indeed, compared with the follies and passions of mankind, which, we must admit, almost entirely control our human destinies, in great things and small. Yet the works of the Understanding outlast the noisy bustling generations and spread light and warmth across the centuries.

❧

10. Man is a peculiar being trying to understand his uniqueness. What he seeks to understand is not his animality but his humanity. He is not in search of his origins, he is in search of his destiny.

ตรง

11. Knowing becomes understanding only when it embraces the beginning, the continuation, and the end.

ตรง

12. Surely we would grow a great deal more swiftly if we could only understand life. If, toward its close, we could look back and see that we have grown in understanding, patience,

sympathy, tolerance, then surely we have not lived in vain; for these are "treasures in heaven" which we *can* take away with us through the gateway of death and bring back again with us through the gateway of the next birth.

๑๑

13. For him who has perception, a mere sign is enough. For him who does not really heed, a thousand explanations are not enough.

๑๑

14. He who would understand the Plains must ascend the Eternal Hills, where a man's eyes scan Infinity. But he

who would make use of understanding must descend to the Plains, where Past and Future meet and men have need of him.

෨෨

15. Socrates said that understanding must be coaxed or persuaded to come forth out of its hidden retreats within the soul. . . . We never release man by pressing our opinions upon him, even if those opinions are themselves true. We must lure a reluctant consciousness to reveal its own purposes, thus leading the creature to a condition of sufficiency.

෨෨

16. There is beauty in understanding, and understanding springs only from an understanding heart, paradoxical as that may sound at first hearing. It is the understanding heart that has vision.

ᖇᕼ

17. You will understand something of the wonders and mysteries of the universe, when you know that things that seem evil from the side of form are good from the side of life; all that happens is working for the best.

ᖇᕼ

18. In each man is a spark able to kindle new fires of human progress, new light

for the human spirit. . . . When enough
of these fires are burning, they create a
new dawn of spiritual understanding;
the flame of a great people is formed.

〰

19. I have an understanding with the hills
    At evening when the slanted radiance
        fills
    Their hollows, and the great winds let
        them be.
    And they are quiet and look down at
        me.

〰

20. He who would have understanding
    must seek where others do not seek,
    or perchance disdain to seek. He must

find where others have failed to find. He must explore where others have explored in vain.

∾

21. The eye of the understanding is like the eye of the sense; for as you may see great objects through small crannies or holes, so you may see great axioms of nature through small and contemptible instances.

∾

22. ... it is significant for the spiritual attitude of Buddhism that it regards right understanding as the first step on the path of liberation, without

which neither morality nor concentration can have any value.

❧

23. I shall light a candle of understanding in thine heart, which shall not be put out.

❧

24. There must be understanding as well as feeling. Both are necessary. When you have these two conjoined and sympathetically co-operating, you have the Sage, the Seer.

❧

25. I hold myself indebted to anyone
from whose enlightened understanding another ray of knowledge com-
municates to mine. Really to inform
the mind is to correct and enlarge the
heart.

∾

26. Salih of Qazwin taught his disciples:
"Whoever knocks at the door
continually, it will be opened
to him."
Rabia, hearing him one day, said:
"How long will you say:
'It will be opened'? The door
has never been shut."

∾

27. In regard to knowledge of myself I am what I seek to know.... Understanding of man is derived from self-understanding, and one can never remain aloof from one's own self.

⚮

28. Another spiritual faculty is the awakened Understanding: the faculty which enables you to discriminate between thoughts and thoughts, things and things, to know one from the other.... Understanding is of the very nature of the Heart of the Universe.

⚮

29. When you understand life, life becomes bearable; and never till you

understand it will it cease to be a burden grievous to be borne; but when you understand it, everything changes.

❧

30. You will in time, by following the inner pathway of self-knowledge, grow so greatly in understanding and inner vision, that your eyes will take in ranges and sweeps of inner light, unveiling to you the most awful, because the holiest and the most beautiful, mysteries of the boundless Universe.

December

HAPPINESS

1. The problem is not a problem of happiness, which is everyone's birthright. Everyone believes he is entitled to happiness. He questions only, when there is pain, why there should be that pain. The problem is a problem of sorrow or suffering, as stated by the lord Buddha in His wisdom long ago. Sorrow and suffering are the denial of life by the limitation that is put upon it.

ॐ

2. The human heart is perfectly right in obeying the instinct which drives it

to try to secure happiness ... it does not come into its own until it comes into this recognition of that which underlies its own self.

∾

3. The secret of human happiness in this world is to live always in tune with the song of Life, to keep the outer self of action, heart, mind, and motive always in tune with the Inner Self, which is ever at one with the Supreme Self, the Lord of All.

∾

4. Every one of these hundreds of millions of human beings is in some form seeking happiness. Not one is altogether noble nor altogether trust-

worthy nor altogether consistent; and not one is altogether vile. Not a single one but has at one time wept.

∽

5. By true acceptance, the disciple comes into oneness of spirit with the over-ruling Soul; and, since the own-nature of the Soul is being, happiness, bliss, he comes thereby into happiness supreme.

∽

6. Happiness is a sunbeam which may pass through a thousand bosoms without losing a particle of its original ray; nay, when it strikes on a kindred heart, like the converged light on a mirror, it reflects itself with redoubled

brightness. It is not perfected till it is shared.

❧

7. The problem of happiness is . . . the most elusive problem of life, but after all is said and done about culture and progress, it should remain the primary concern of mankind's highest wisdom to solve it.

❧

8. No one can *give* happiness to another; together people can create it. True happiness in any relationship can persist only so long as the persons involved in that relationship continue to be creative channels for life.

❧

9. The state of highest happiness is that in which the consciousness is universal, free as the air, and can identify itself with every passing movement, the flight of a bird, the quivering leaf, the care of an ant, the smiles and tears of other human beings, all in an instant.

∾

10. We shall come closer to finding inner happiness and steadiness if we do not think of our spiritual life and our practical life as existing without connection. These two realms, the practical and the spiritual, are intercommunicating rooms in the house of life. The door must be kept open between them.

∾

11. The truth . . . is that, if a man puts himself into accord with the divine law, happiness is the result of such harmony. The error is to identify worldly success with happiness, and to disregard the element of time.

~

12. The more man progresses, the more radiant and joyful will be his consciousness. Happiness, indeed, may be called a characteristic of progress. In the course of its development it becomes more and more sublime, until it grows into that serenity which radiates from the face to the Enlightened One with that subtle smile in which wisdom, compassion, and all-embracing love are mingled.

~

13. Happiness is in fullness of life. Life is consciousness and exists at all levels, mental, emotional, and physical. Fullness implies therefore fullness of realization, the realization of all ideals, truth, beauty, and goodness, the harmonization of thought and action.

∞

14. . . . we choose happiness for itself, and never with a view to anything further; whereas we choose honor, pleasure, intellect . . . because we believe that through them we shall be made happy.

∞

15. If you are yourself full of happiness, that radiant joy is poured upon all

who come near you, and you become a veritable sun.

∾

16. Only when we live with abandonment of self, with absolute self-surrender, with no element of inhibition, no urge, no obstruction, shall we know what freedom means, and thus experience the truest happiness.

∾

17. There can be no abiding happiness without balanced growth. The lasting joy of fulfillment can spring only from the integration of one's total personality . . . . True happiness is a

function of one's total desire-nature
organized into a self-coherent whole.

❧

18. The foolish man seeks happiness in
the distance; the wise grows it under
his feet.

❧

19. It is only a poor sort of happiness
that could ever come by caring very
much about our own narrow pleas-
ures. We can only have the highest
happiness, such as goes along with true
greatness, by having wide thoughts and
much feeling for the rest of the world
as well as ourselves; and this sort of
happiness often brings so much pain

with it that we can only tell it from pain by its being what we would choose before everything else, because our souls see it is good.

๑ด

20. Happiness . . . does not need to be pursued or sought, and is the *free* expression of life, which in the case of the human being is possible only when the workings of his nature, his mind, are unconditioned by its own past.

๑ด

21. Let us seek the happiness in others; but for ourselves—perfection—whether it bring us happiness or pain. To achieve perfection in yourself and

happiness in others, "so act as to treat humanity, whether in thine own person or in that of another, in every case as an end, never as a means."

❧

22. We live happily indeed, not hating those who hate us!

We live happily indeed, free from greed among the greedy!

We live happily indeed, though we call nothing our own!

He who has given up both victory and defeat, he, the contented, is happy.

❧

23. Happy are they who discover their chord in the Grand Symphony [of

life] and try always to play it, live it, sing it in tune with the Archetypal pattern, the scheme of life and form of the universe of which they are a part.

∾

24. Happiness in this world, when it comes, comes incidentally. Make it the object of pursuit, and it leads us a wild-goose chase and is never attained. Follow some other object, and very possibly we may find that we have caught happiness without dreaming of it.

∾

25. The deep-rooted yearning for Happiness, planted in every sentient creature, spurs him to place himself at last

in harmony with law, that is, to do the Right, to refuse to do the Wrong.

❧

26. This is the true joy of life—the being used for a purpose recognized by yourself as a mighty one, the being thoroughly worn out before you are thrown to the scrap-heap; the being a force of nature instead of a feverish, selfish clod of ailments and grievances.

❧

27. There is but one way to tranquillity of mind and happiness; let this, therefore, be always ready at hand with thee, both when thou wakest early in the morning, and all the day

long, and when thou goest late to sleep, to account no external things thine own, but commit all these to God.

∽

28. In vain do they talk of happiness who never subdued an impulse in obedience to a principle. He who never sacrificed a present to a future good, or a personal to a general one, can speak of happiness only as the blind do of colors.

∽

29. We have no more right to consume happiness without producing it than

to consume wealth without producing
it.

❦

30. The happiness of life is made up of
minute fractions—the little soon-for-
gotten charities of a kiss or smile, a
kind look, a heartfelt compliment, and
the countless infinitesimals of pleasura-
ble and genial feeling.

❦

31. Happiness is a pure and simple cup
that is devoid both of excitation and
opiates, of the poison of an ever-recur-
ring thirst, as well as the oblivion of
indifference to others, a cup that ever
measures full.

SOURCES OF THE MEDITATIONS

(*Note:* When a specific book and author have been cited more than once in the meditations for a month, the author's name and the full title of the book or essay (if known) will be given the first time; immediately following references from the same source will be idicated by "Ibid"; subsequent references in the same month will be designated by the author's last name and the key word(s) of the title.)

JANUARY
1. N. Sri Ram, *Thoughts for Aspirants*
2. Antionette K. Gordon, tr., *Hundred Thousand Songs of Milarepa*
3. Kahlil Gibran, *The Prophet*
4. Bradford Smith, *Meditation: The Inward Art*
5. Joy Mills, "The Burden of Freedom," *The American Theosophist*
6. Arthur W. Osborn, "Freedom from What?" Ibid.
7. Will Durant (of Kant), *The Story of Philosophy*
8. George S. Arundale, *Freedom and Friendship*
9. Geoffrey Farthing, "The Bondage of Being," *Am. Theos.*
10. Laurence J. Bendit, "Evolution into Freedom," ibid.
11. Sri Madhava Ashish, "Bondage as Freedom," ibid.
12. Clarence R. Pedersen, "The Chains of Living," ibid.

SOURCES

13. Charles Johnston, tr., *The Crest Jewel of Wisdom* (Shankaracharya)
14. James S. Perkins, "Dimensions of Freedom," *Am. Theos.*
15. George E. Linton, "Ancient Founts of Inspiration," ibid.
16. N. Sri Ram, *On the Watchtower*
17. Mills, "Freedom," *Am. Theos.*
18. Sir Henry Jones, *A Faith that Inquires*
19. I. K. Taimni, "Freedom—Real and Unreal," *Am. Theos.*
20. Virginia Hanson, "Freedom and Self-Knowledge," ibid.
21. Osborn, "Freedom," ibid.
22. Perkins, "Dimensions," ibid.
23. Sri Ram, *Thoughts*
24. Jones, *Faith*
25. Mills, "Freedom," *Am. Theos.*
26. Pedersen, "Chains," ibid.
27. Sri Ram, *Watchtower*
28. Taimni, "Freedom," *Am. Theos.*
29. Ashish, "Bondage," ibid.
30. Sri Ram, *Seeking Wisdom*
31. Elsie Morgan, *Your Own Path*

FEBRUARY
1. H. P. Blavatsky, *The Voice of the Silence*
2. N. Sri Ram, *Thoughts for Aspirants*
3. Joshua Loth Liebman, *Peace of Mind*

4. Bert Finck, *Musings on the Lounge*
5. Henry Alonzo Myers, *Are Men Equal?*
6. Marcus Aurelius, *Meditations*
7. C. Jinarajadasa, *The Divine Vision*
8. Lam. 3:22-23
9. George S. Arundale, *Gods in the Becoming*
10. G. de Purucker, *Golden Precepts*
11. Clara Codd, *The Ageless Wisdom of Life*
12. Codd, ibid.
13. Charles Henry Mackintosh, *I Looked on Life*
14. Purucker, *Precepts*
15. Thomas Wolfe, *The Web and the Rock*
16. Purucker, *Precepts*
17. Abraham Heschel, *Who is Man?*
18. Henry Steel Olcott, *Old Diary Leaves,* I
19, Purucker, *Precepts*
20. Annie Besant,. *Doctrine of the Heart*
21. Antoinette K. Gordon, tr., *Hundred Thousand Songs of Milarepa*
22. Purucker, *Precepts*
23. Ibid.
24. Nicholas Caussin
25. A. T. Barker, ed., *The Mahatma Letters to A. P. Sinnett*
26. Purucker, *Precepts*
27. Heschel, *Man*
28. Blavatsky, *Voice*
29. *Jubilee*

MARCH

1. Gardner Murphy, *Main Currents in Modern Thought*
2. Sir Isaac Newton, Brewster's *Memoirs of Newton*
3. J. J. van der Leeuw, *The Conquest of Illusion*
4. Paul Brunton, *The Wisdom of the Overself*
5. N. Sri Ram, *The Human Interest*
6. G. de Purucker, *Golden Precepts*
7. Virginia Hanson, "Freedom and Self-Knowledge," *The American Theosophist*
8. Clara Codd, *The Ageless Wisdom of Life*
9. F. W. Ruckstull, *Great Works of Art*
10. Sri Aurobindo, *Bases of Yoga*
11. N. Sri Ram, *An Approach to Reality*
12. Basil King, *The Conquest of Fear*
13. Indries Shah, *The Way of the Sufi*
14. William James, *Lectures*
15. Sir Henry Jones, *A Faith that Inquires*
16. Francis Bacon, "Of Truth," *Essays*
17. Hans-Ulrich Rieker, *The Secret of Meditation*
18. Will Durant, *The Story of Philosophy*
19. C. G. Jung, "The Psychology of the Transference," *The Practice of Psychotherapy*
20. Van der Leeuw, *Conquest*
21. Sri Ram, *Approach*
22. Rieker, *Meditation*
23. Sri Ram, *Human*
24. Sri Aurobindo, *Bases of Yoga*
25. Van der Leeuw, *Conquest*
26. Sri Ram, *Approach*
27. Thomas Carlyle, *Heroes and Hero Worship*

28. Sri Ram, *Approach*
29. Brunton, *The Secret Path*
30. Sri Ram, *Approach*
31. Sri Ram, *Speaking Wisdom*

APRIL

1. N. Sri Ram, *Thoughts for Aspirants*
2. Paramahansa Yogananda, *Metaphysical Meditations*
3. Duchesne-Guillemin, *The Hymns of Zarathustra*
4. Pendle Hill & Harper, *The Cloud of Unknowing*
5. Josephine Ransom, *Self-Realization through Yoga and Mysticism*
6. N. Sri Ram, *The Human Interest*
7. Annie Besant, tr., *The Bhagavad Gita*
8. Brother Lawrence, *The Practice of the Presence of God*
9. Pendle Hill & Harper, *Unknowing*
10. Annie Besant, *The Inner Government of the World*
11. Yoganada, *Meditations*
12. C. Jinarajadasa, *First Principles of Theosophy*
13. Sri Ram, *Human*
14. C. W. Leadbeater, *The Masters and the Path*
15. Lev. 27:28
16. Besant, tr., *Gita*
17. Aurobindo, *Yoga*
18. Sri Ram, *Human*
19. Matt. 22:34-40
20. Annie Besant, *Laws of the Higher Life*

21. Author unknown, *The Eternal Wisdom*
22. A. J. Arberry, *Sufism*
23. Besant, tr., *Gita*
24. Lawrence, *Practice*
25. Sri Ram, *Human*
26. Pendle Hill & Harper, *Unknowing*
27. Duchesne-Guillemin, *Hymns*
28. Lawrence, *Practice*
29. Besant, tr., *Gita*
30. Pendle Hill & Harper, *Unknowing*

MAY

1. N. Sri Ram, *An Approach to Reality*
2. George S. Arundale, *Mt. Everest*
3. Will Durant, *The Story of Philosophy*
4. F. G. Montagu Powell, *Studies in the Lesser Mysteries*
5. H. P. Blavatsky, *Isis Unveiled, I*
6. Arundale, *Everest*
7. Claude Bragdon, *Delphic Woman*
8. J. J. van der Leeuw, *The Conquest of Illusion*
9. William Wordsworth, "The Excursion"
10. Sri Ram, *Approach*
11. J. Krishnamurti, *The Kingdom of Happiness*
12. Lama Anagarika Govinda, *The Psychological Attitude of Early Buddhist Philosophy*
13. Ernest Wood, *Intuition of the Will*
14. Arundale, *Everest*

15. Dag Hammerskjold, *Markings*
16. A. T. Barker, ed., *The Mahatma Letters to A. P. Sinnett*
17. Plotinus
18. G. de Purucker, *Golden Precepts*
19. Paul Brunton, *Wisdom of the Overself*
20. Sir Henry Jones, *A Faith that Inquires*
21. Arundale, *Everest*
22. C. Jinarajadasa, ed., *Letters from the Masters of the Wisdom*, II
23. Van der Leeuw, *Conquest*
24. Sri Ram, *Approach*
25. Arundale, *Everest*
26. Barker, ed., *Mahatma Letters*
27. Roy Mitchell, *Exile of the Saul*
28. Arundale, *Everest*
29. Van der Leeuw, *Conquest*
30. Annie Basant, *In the Outer Court*
31. Sri Ram, *Approach*

JUNE

1. N. Sri Ram, *An Approach to Reality*
2. George S. Arundale, *You*
3. George Santayana, *The Sense of Beauty*
4. Bradford Smith, *Meditation: The Inward Art*
5. Oscar Wilde, *The Picture of Dorian Gray*
6. N. Sri Ram, *The Human Interest*
7. Ernest Wood, *The Seven Rays*

SOURCES

8. Ralph Waldo Emerson, "The Poet," *Essays*
9. Louis Anspacher, *Challenge of the Unknown*
10. Manly P. Hall, *The Mystical Christ*
11. Plato, *The Republic*
12. C. Jinarajadasa, *Karma-less-ness*
13. Vera Brittain, *Testament of Youth*
14. Kahlil Gibran, *The Prophet*
15. Smith, *Meditation*
16. G. de Purucker, *Golden Precepts*
17. Santayana, *Beauty*
18. Dag Hammerskjold, *Markings*
19. C. Jinarajadasa, *Gods in Chains*
20. Sri Ram, *Human*
21. F. W. Ruckstull, *Great Works of Art*
22. Emerson, "Art," *Essays*
23. Jinarajadasa, *Karma-less-ness*
24. Marcus Aurelius, *Meditations*
25. L. M. Little, "Fairy Gold"
26. Sri Ram, *Human*
27. Sir Henry Jones, *A Faith that Inquires*
28. Ruckstull, *Works*
29. Smith, *Meditation*
30. Sri Ram, *Approach*

JULY

1. H. P. Blavatsky, *The Key to Theosophy*
2. H. M. Tomlinson
3. Clara Codd, *The Ageless Wisdom of Life*

4. N. Sri Ram, *Seeking Wisdom*
5. Annie Besant, *Some Difficulties of the Inner Life*
6. G. de Purucker, *Golden Precepts*
7. F. S. Marvin, *History at Oxford,* Introduction
8. Thornton Wilder, *The Ides of March*
9. Basil King, *The Conquest of Fear*
10. Sri Aurobindo, *Bases of Yoga*
11. Harry Emerson Fosdick, *Successful Christian Living*
12. Vera Brittain, *Testament of Youth*
13. Codd, *Wisdom*
14. I. A. R. Wylie, "The Quest of Our Lives," *Readers Digest*
15. Franz Werfel, *The Forty Days of Musa Dagh*
16. Annie Besant, quoted in Codd, *Wisdom*
17. William Allen White, *Autobiography*
18. Thomas Carlyle, *Heroes and Hero Worship*
19. King, *Conquest*
20. Annie Besant and C. W. Leadbeater, *Talks on the Path of Occultism*
21. Dag Hammerskjold, *Markings*
22. Victor Hugo, *Les Miserables*
23. Wylie, "Quest"
24. Besant and Leadbeater, *Talks*
25. Wilder, *Ides*
26. Annie Besant, *Initiation*
27. Wilder, *Ides*
28. Joseph R. Sizoo, *Preaching Unashamed*
29. King, *Conquest*
30. Annie Besant, *The Functions of the Gods*
31. N. Sri Ram, *The Human Interest*

SOURCES

AUGUST

1. N. Sri Ram, *Thoughts for Aspirants*
2. Brother Lawrence, *The Practice of the Presence of God*
3. Thomas a' Kempis, *Imitation of Christ*
4. Ik Marvel, *Reveries of a Bachelor*
5. Micah 6:8
6. Witter Bynner, tr., *The Way of Life* (Lao-tzu)
7. John Macy, *The Story of the World's Literature*
8. Dag Hammerskjold, *Markings*
9. St. Francis of Assisi, *The Councils of the Holy Father*
10. Lawrence, *Practice*
11. Sri Ram, *Thoughts*
12. Thomas Moore, *The Loves of the Angels*
13. Matt. 23:22
14. Harvey Cushing, *Life of Sir William Osler*
15. Alfred Lord Tennyson, *Idylls of the King*
16. Sri Ram, *Thoughts*
17. Charles H. Spurgeon, *Gleanings Among the Sheaves*
18. Hammerskjold, *Markings*
19. N. Sri Ram, *Seeking Wisdom*
20. Euripides, *The Bacchae*
21. T. S. Eliot, *Four Quartets*
22. Idries Shah, *The Way of the Sufi*
23. Cicero, *De Officiis*
24. Walter Malone, *The Humbler Poets*
25. Hammerskjold, *Markings*
26. Rudyard Kipling, "Recessional"

27. Sri Ram, *Wisdom*
28. A. J. Arberry, *Sufism*
29. Hammerskjold, *Markings*
30. T. S. Eliot, *Shakespeare and the Stoicism of Seneca*
31. Sri Ram, *Thoughts*

SEPTEMBER

1. N. Sri Ram, *An Approach to Reality*
2. John Henry Strong, *Jesus, the Man of Prayer*
3. N. Sri Ram, *Thoughts for Aspirants*
4. Haridas Chaudhuri, *Mastering the Problems of Living*
5. G. de Purucker, *Golden Precepts*
6. Annie Besant, *Theosophy and Life's Deeper Problems*
7. Hans-Ulrich Rieker, *The Secret of Meditation*
8. Starr Dailey, *Release*
9. Sri Ram, *Approach*
10. Albert Einstein, *Out of My Later Years*
11. Clara Codd, *The Ageless Wisdom of Life*
12. J. J. van der Leeuw, *The Conquest of Illusion*
13. St. Paul, Col. 4:8
14. Annie Besant, *Wisdom of the Upanishads*
15. *The Dhammapada*
16. John Ruskin
17. Sri Ram, *Thoughts*
18. Purucker, *Precepts*
19. Charles Henry Mackintosh, *I Looked on Life*

SOURCES

20. Lama Anagarika Govinda, *The Psychological Attitude of Early Buddhist Philosophy*
21. Bradford Smith, *Meditation: The Inward Art*
22. Codd, *Wisdom*
23. Annie Besant, *Initiation*
24. Henry C. Link, *My Return to Religion*
25. Jolande Jacobi, *The Way of Individuation*
26. Dag Hammerskjold, *Markings*
27. A. T. Barker, ed., *The Mahatma Letters to A. P. Sinnett*
28. Haridas Chaudhuri, *Problems*
29. Govinda, *Attitudes*
30. Sri Ram, *Thoughts*

OCTOBER

1. N. Sri Ram, *Seeking Wisdom*
2. H. P. Blavatsky, *The Key to Theosophy*
3. Starr Dailey, *Release*
4. N. Sri Ram, *Thoughts for Aspirants*
5. Charles Johnston tr., *Yoga Sutras of Patanjali*
6. Annie Besant, tr., *The Bhagavad Gita*, Preface
7. Sri Ram, *Thoughts*
8. Basil King, *The Conquest of Fear*
9. G. de Purucker, *Golden Precepts*
10. Sri Ram, *Thoughts*
11. Aldous Huxley, *Jesting Pilate*
12. H. P. Blavatsky, *The Secret Doctrine, 5*
13. Sri Ram, *Wisdom*

14. Plato, *The Republic*
15. Annie Besant, *In the Outer Court*
16. H. P. Blavatsky, quoted by Clara Codd, *The Ageless Wisdom of Life*
17. Sri Ram, *Thoughts*
18. Purucker, *Precepts*
19. Codd, *Wisdom*
20. Sri Ram, *Wisdom*
21. Haridas Chaudhuri, *Mastering the Problems of Living*
22. Annie Besant, tr. *The Bhagavad Gita,* Introduction
23. Sri Ram, *Thoughts*
24. Blavatsky, *Key*
25. Sri Ram, *Thoughts*
26. Chaudhuri, *Problems*
27. N. P. Blavatsky, *Isis Unveiled*
28. Sri Ram, *Thoughts*
29. Blavatsky, *Isis*
30. Chaudhuri, *Problems*
31. Sri Ram, *Thoughts*

NOVEMBER

1. George S. Arundale, *Understanding is Happiness*
2. Ibid.
3. Ibid.
4. Ibid.
5. Ibid.

SOURCES

6. Ibid.
7. Ibid.
8. N. Sri Ram, *Thoughts for Aspirants*
9. Albert Einstein, *Out of My Later Years*
10. Abraham Heschel, *Who is Man?*
11. Jolande Jacobi, *The Way of Individuation*
12. Clara Codd, *The Ageless Wisdom of Life*
13. Idries Shah, *The Way of the Sufi*
14. Talbot Mundy, *OM*
15. Manly P. Hall, "The Mystical Figures of Jakob Boehme"
16. G. de Purucker, *Golden Precepts*
17. Annie Besant, *Dharma*
18. Charles A. Lindbergh, *Of Flight and Life*
19. Grace Hazard Conkling, *After Sunset*
20. Arundale, *Understanding, The Light-Bringer*
21. Francis Bacon, *Essays*
22. Lama Anagarika Govinda, *The Psychological Attitude of Early Buddhist Philosophy*
23. Esdras, The Apocrypha
24. Purucker, *Precepts*
25. Junius
26. Shah, *Sufi*
27. Heschel, *Man*
28. Purucker, *Precepts*
29. Annie Besant, *The Field of Work of The Theosophical Society*
30. Purucker, *Precepts*

DECEMBER

1. N. Sri Ram, *The Human Interest*
2. Paul Brunton, *Wisdom of the Overself*
3. Goeffrey Hodson, *Occult Powers in Nature and in Man*
4. Herbert George Wells
5. Charles Johnston, tr., *Yoga Sutras of Patanjali*
6. Jane Porter
7. Lin Yutang, *My Country and My People*
8. Anonymous
9. Sri Ram, *Human*
10. Thomas Cole, *Standing up to Life*
11. Annie Besant, *A Study in Karma*
12. Lama Anagarika Govinda, *The Psychological Attitude of Early Buddhist Philosophy*
13. Sri Ram, *Human*
14. Will Durant (of Aristotle), *The Story of Philosophy*
15. C. W. Leadbeater, *The Hidden Side of Things*
16. N. Sri Ram, *Thoughts for Aspirants*
17. Haridas Chaudhuri, *Mastering the Problems of Living*
18. James Oppenheim
19. George Eliot
20. Sri Ram, *Human*
21. Will Durant (of Kant), *The Story of Philosophy*
22. F. Max Müeller, tr., *The Dhammapada*
23. Geoffrey Hodson, *Occult Powers*
24. Nathaniel Hawthorne, *American Note Book*
25. Annie Besant, *Theosophy*

SOURCES

26. George Bernard Shaw
27. Epictetus
28. Horace Mann
29. George Bernard Shaw, *Candida*
30. Samuel Taylor Coleridge, *The Friend*
31. Sri Ram, *Thoughts*

QUEST BOOKS

This book is one of the Quest Miniature Series, a special imprint of the Theosophical Publishing House. Other Quest Miniatures are:

At the Feet of the Master *by Alcyone*
The Buddhist Catechism *by Henry Steel Olcott*
Circle of Wisdom *by Helena Petrovna Blavatsky*
Fragments *by C. Jinarajadasa*
From the Outer Court to the Inner Sanctum
                              by Annie Besant
Golden Precepts *by G. de Purucker*
Hymn of Jesus *by G. R. S. Mead*
Light of the Path *by Mabel Collins*
Natural Man *by Henry David Thoreau*
Reflective Meditation *by Kay Mouradian*
The Secret of Happiness *by Irving S. Cooper*
The Song Celestial *by Sir Edwin Arnold*
Tao *by Charles H. Mackintosh*
Thoughts for Aspirants *by N. Sri Ram*
Trust Yourself to Life *by Clara Codd*
Voice of the Silence *by Helena Petrovna Blavatsky*

**Available from
QUEST BOOKS
306 West Geneva Road
Wheaton, Illinois 60187**